westermann

W0215337

ONE, TWO, FUN!

Workbook 1 / 2

Erarbeitet von
Karen B. Finck, Rheinland-Pfalz
Elke Neudeck, Brandenburg
Ute Schwickert, Rheinland-Pfalz
unter Mitarbeit der Verlagsredaktion

Illustriert von
Juliane Assies, Andrea Dölling, Karoline Kehr,
Oda Ruthe, Friederike Schumann
sowie Iris Blanck, Gabie Hilgert,
Carmen Hochmann, Markus Humbach,
Ulf Marckwort, Isabelle Metzen

CONTENTS

Hello

1

2

3

4

1. Listen. 2. Listen and point. 3. Listen and circle.
4. Say your name.
Diff ⇩ L liest die Hörtexte selbst vor.

CD 1/ 1–3 KV 1, 3
FC 1–7

Colours

1

2

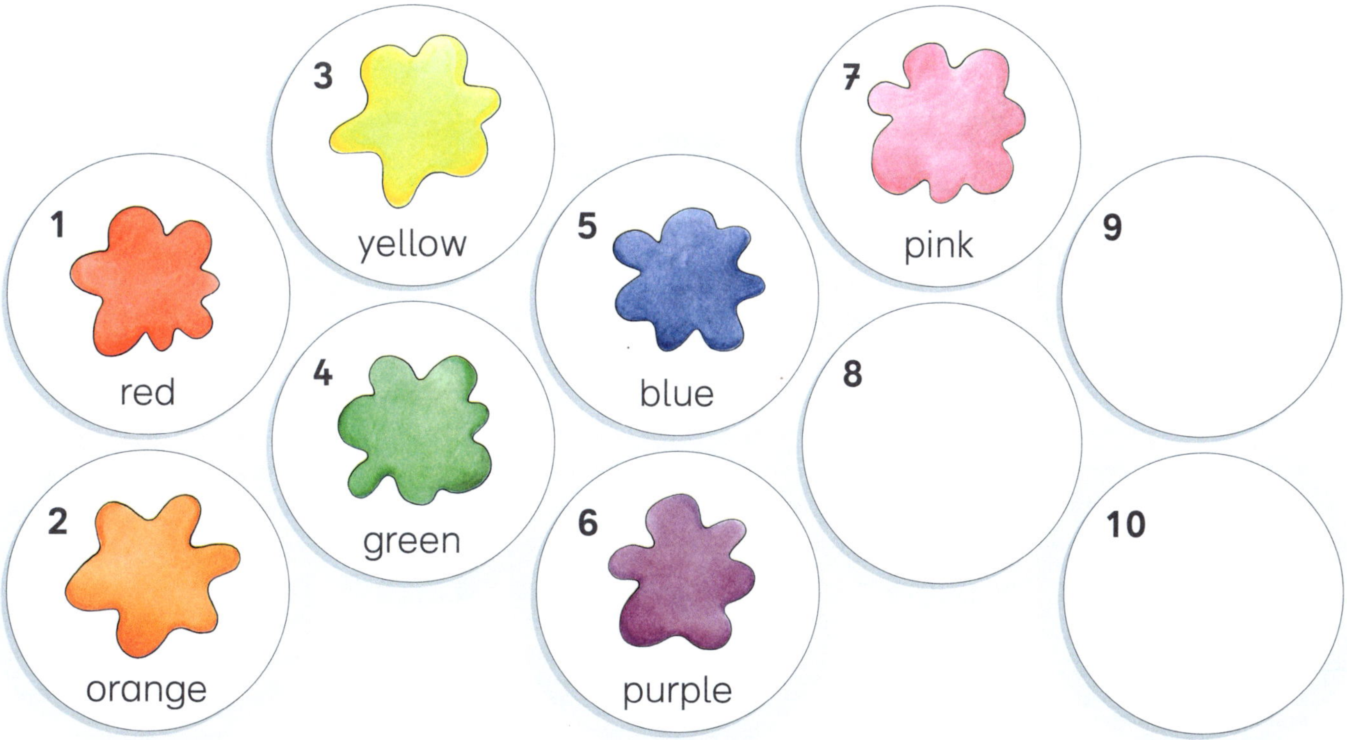

3

4

1. Listen and point. 2. Listen and repeat.
3. Look and colour. 4. Say the lines.
Diff ⇧ SuS gestalten eigene Farbreihen./SuS ergänzen Farben.

KV 1–3
FC/WC 1–7

Song: I can sing a rainbow (Arthur Hamilton)

1

2

3

4

5

Aus rechtlichen Gründen kann zum Lied kein QR-Code angeboten werden.

1. Listen to the song. **2.** Listen again. Colour and draw.
3. Sing the song. **4.** Draw a rainbow. **5.** Present your rainbow.
Diff ⇩ L singt das Lied selbst Wort für Wort vor.

CD 1/ 4–5 **KV** 4
FC/WC 1–7

FLORY'S MAGIC PHOTO ALBUM

Flags and colours

1

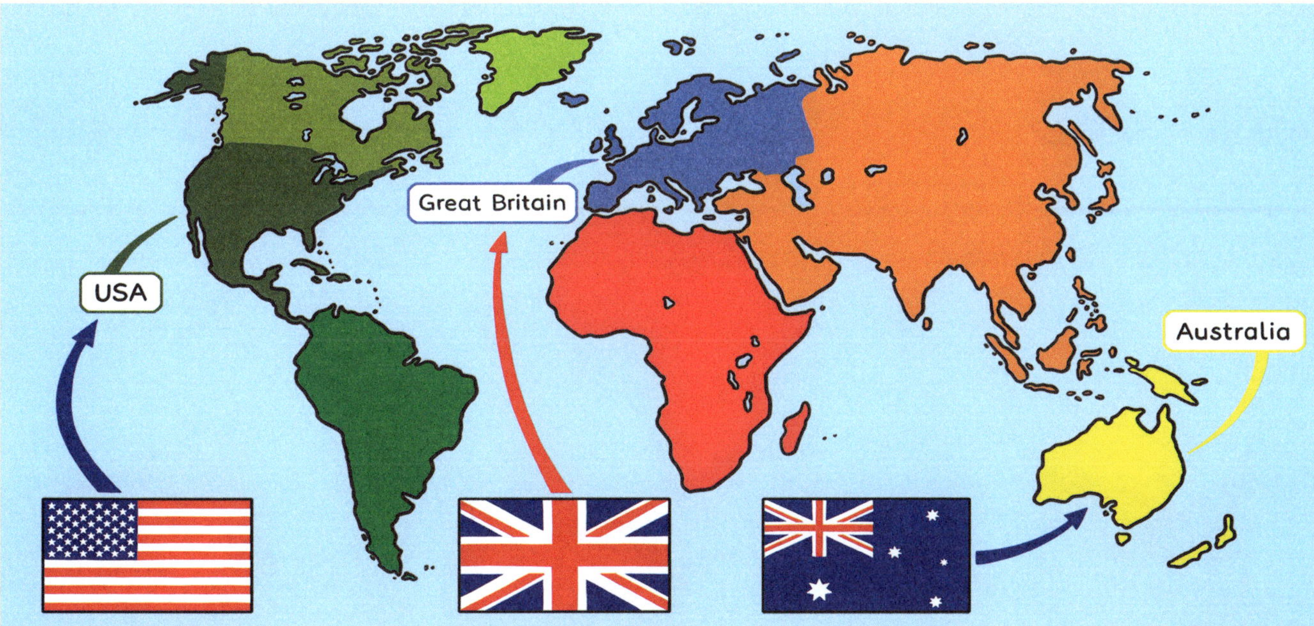

2 **3**

1. Listen. 2. Colour the flags. 3. Listen and point.
Diff ⇧ SuS nennen weitere englischsprachige Länder.
Diff ⇩ L liest die Hörtexte selbst vor.

CD 1/ 6–7 **KV** 3, 4

Favourite colours

1

2

3

1. Listen and match. **2.** What about you? Draw.
3. Talk to your partner.
Diff ⇩ SuS sprechen im Einwortsatz über ihre Lieblingsfarben.

CD 1/ 8 **KV** 5, 102
FC/WC 1 – 7

My parrot

1

1.

2.

3.

4.

5.

6.

2

3

PORTFOLIO SEITE 72

1. Look and make your parrot. **2.** Present your parrot.
3. Decorate your classroom.

KV 6 a-b

At school

1

2

3

1. Listen and point. **2.** Listen and show. **3.** Listen and colour.
Diff ⇧ SuS äußern sich frei zur Illustration.
Diff ⇩ L liest die Hörtexte selbst vor. **Wdh.** colours

CD 1/ 9–11
KV 7, 102
FC 8–15, (1–7)

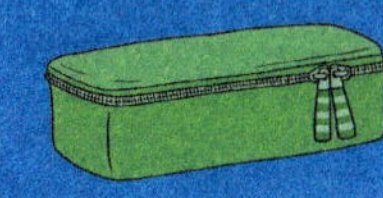

School things

1 (Listen and point) **2** (Listen and repeat)

3 (Listen and circle)

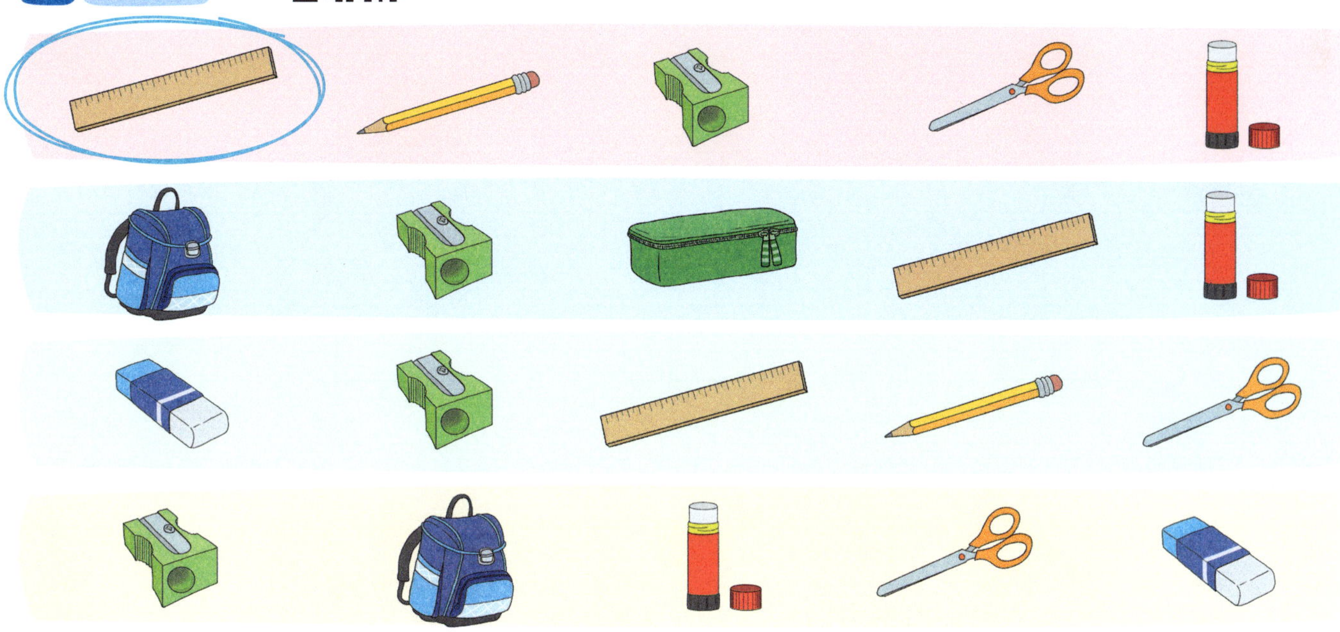

4 (Say the lines)

Rap: One, two, fun!

1

2

3

ONE, TWO, FUN!

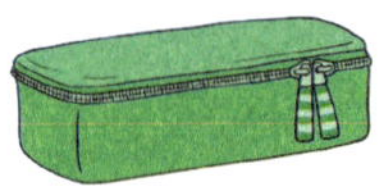  !

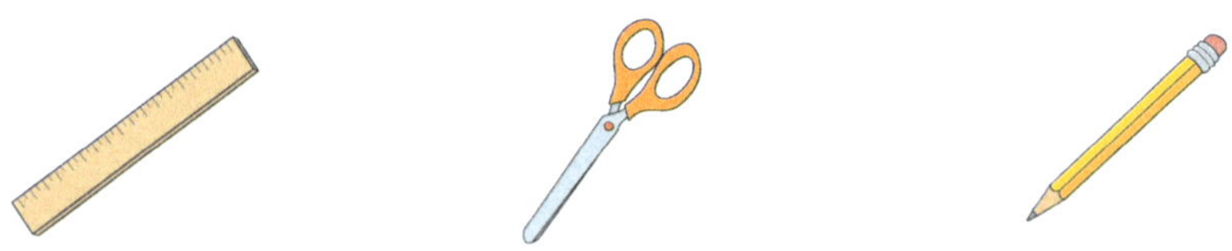

☒ ☐ ☐ !

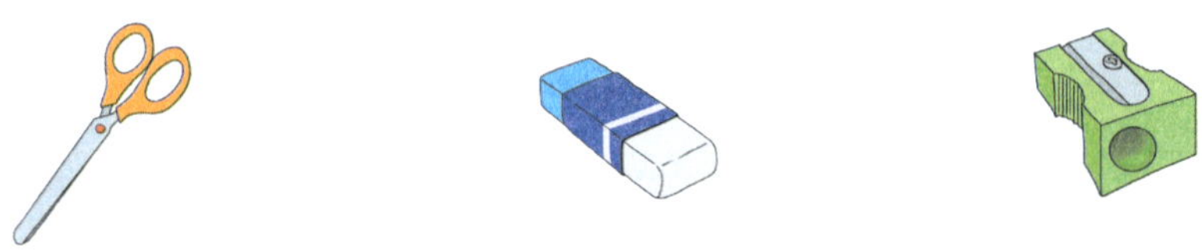

☐ ☐ ☐ !

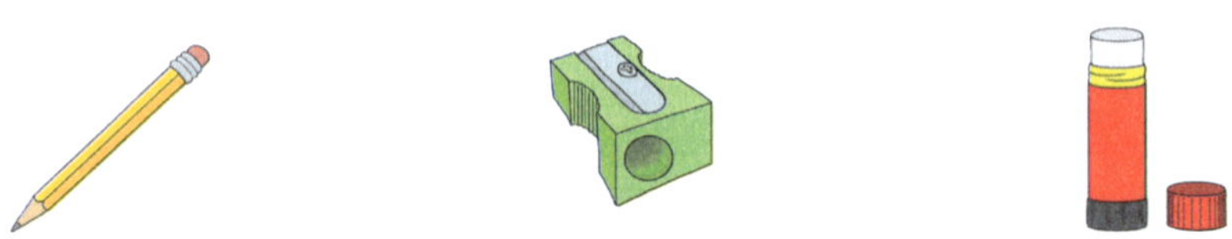

☐ ☐ ☐ !

1. Listen to the song. 2. Listen again and tick. 3. Do the rap.
Diff ⇑ SuS ergänzen weitere Strophen.
Diff ⇓ L trägt den Rap selbst vor.

CD 1/ 13–14
FC/WC 8–14

★ Ich kenne den Schultag von Kindern in England.

FLORY'S MAGIC PHOTO ALBUM

At school in England

1

2

3

1. Listen and look at the pictures. **2.** Listen and colour.
3. Listen and point.
Diff ⇩ L liest die Hörtexte selbst vor. **Wdh.** colours

CD 1/ 15 – 17
KV 11

My pencil case

1

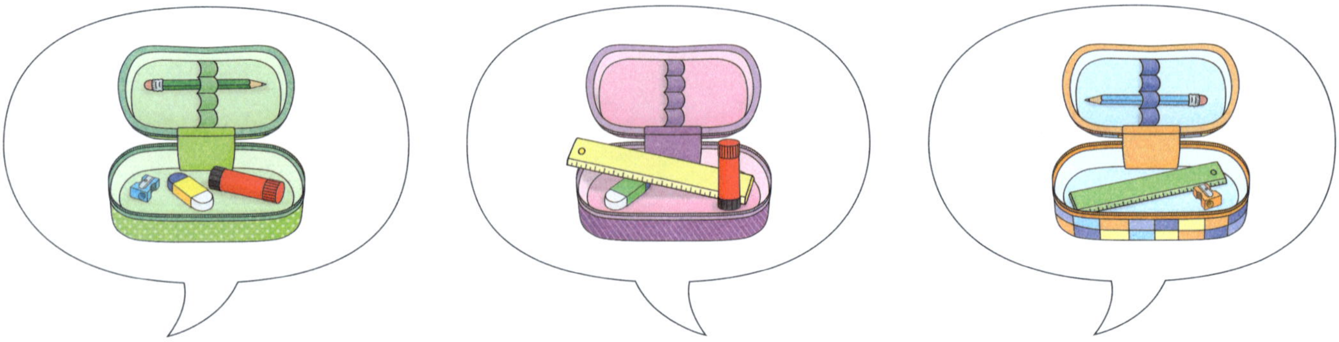

2

3

I've got ...

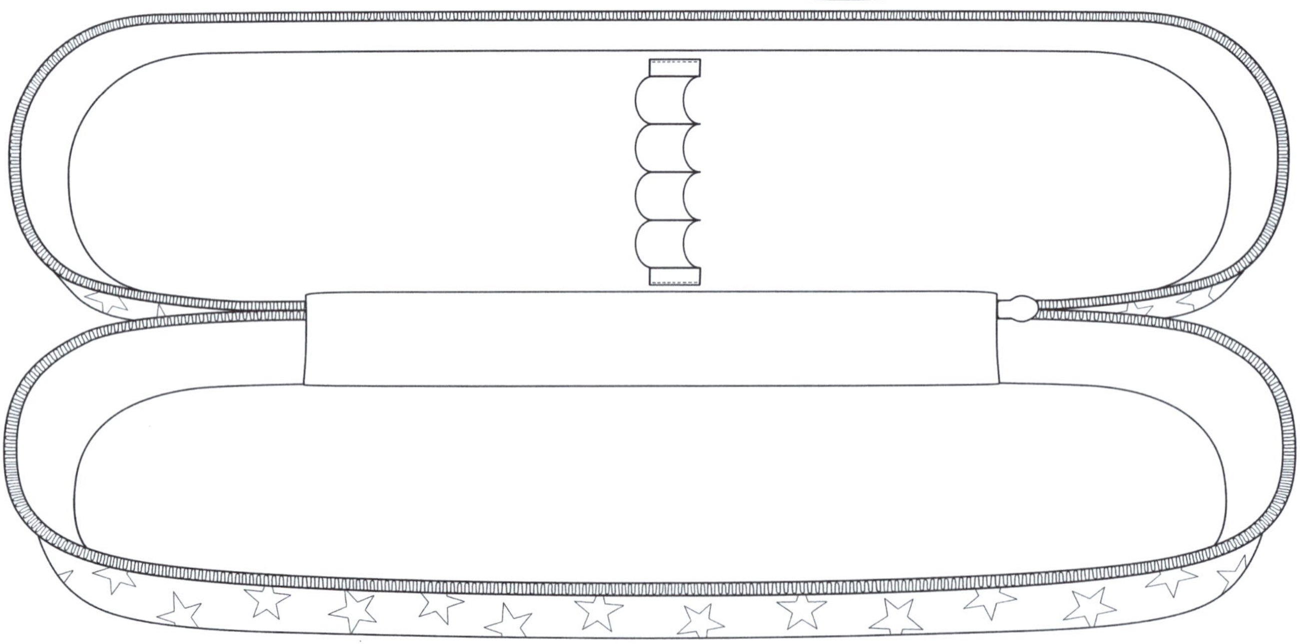

1. Listen and match. 2. What about you? Draw.
3. Present your pencil case. Talk to your partner.
Diff ⇩ SuS präsentieren nur einen Schulgegenstand.

CD 1/ 18
FC/WC 8 – 14

At school – game

1

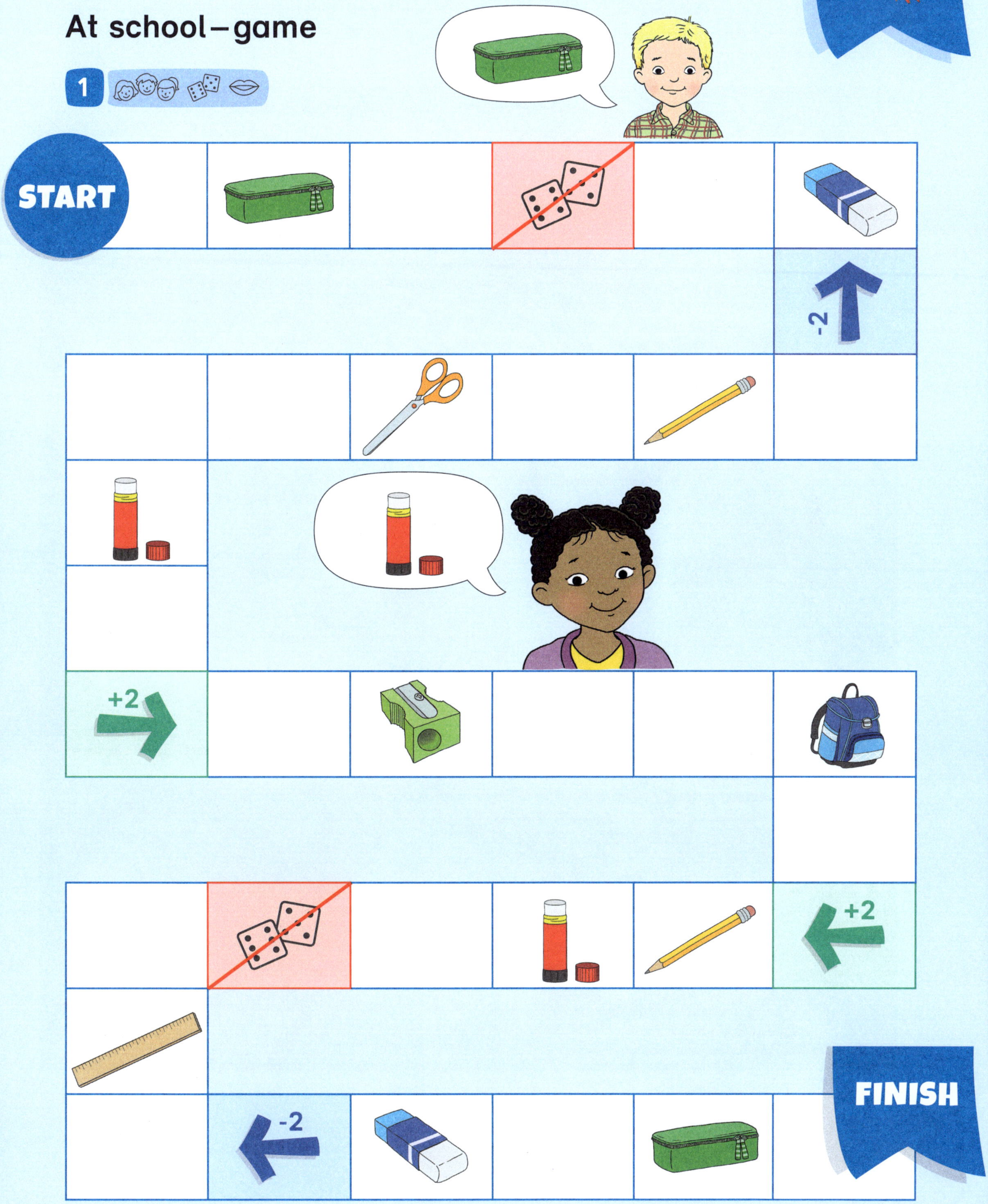

PORTFOLIO SEITE 73

1. Play the game.

Diff ⇑ SuS nennen zusätzlich die Farbe des Gegenstandes.

Diff ⇓ SuS sprechen im Einwortsatz.

KV 9, 12 a-c

FC/WC 8 – 15

Pets

1 2

1. Listen and point. 2. Listen and circle.
Diff ⇧ SuS äußern sich frei zur Illustration.
Diff ⇩ L liest die Hörtexte selbst vor.
Wdh. colours

CD 1/ 19–20
KV 13, 17
FC 16–22, (1–7)

Do you like …?

1 (Listen and point) **2** (Listen and repeat)

3 (Listen and fill in)

	😀	😀	☹		

4 (Ask your partner)

me					
my partner					

Numbers 1 - 6

1

2

1 one

2 two

3 three

4 four

5 five

6 six

3

4

5

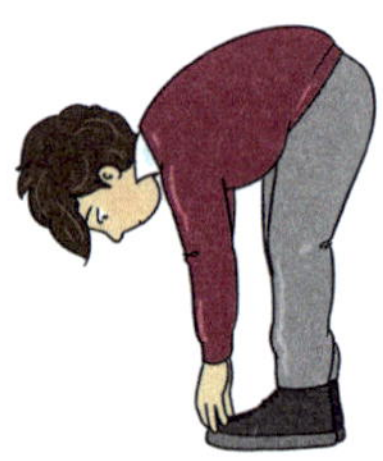

1. Listen and point. **2.** Listen and repeat. **3.** Listen to the rhyme.
4. Listen and fill in the numbers. **5.** Say and do the rhyme.
Diff ⇧ SuS tragen den Reim alleine vor.

CD 1/ 22–23
KV 15, 16, 19
FC/WC 23–28

Rain, rain go away

1 👂

2 👂 ✏

Pets and numbers

1

2

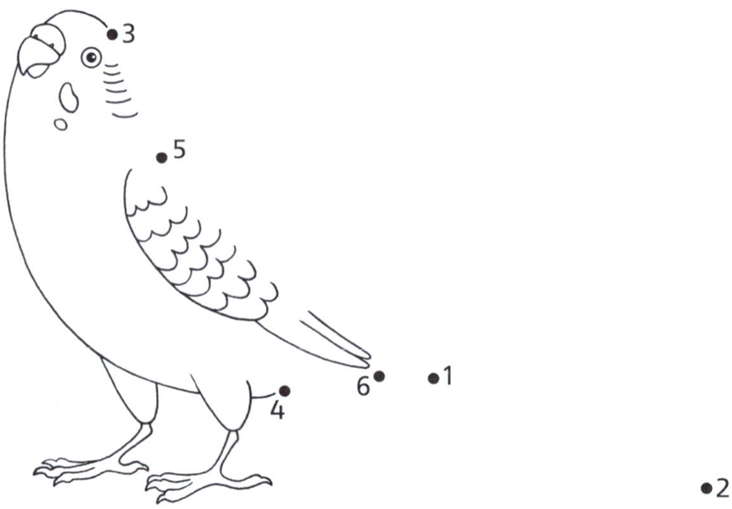

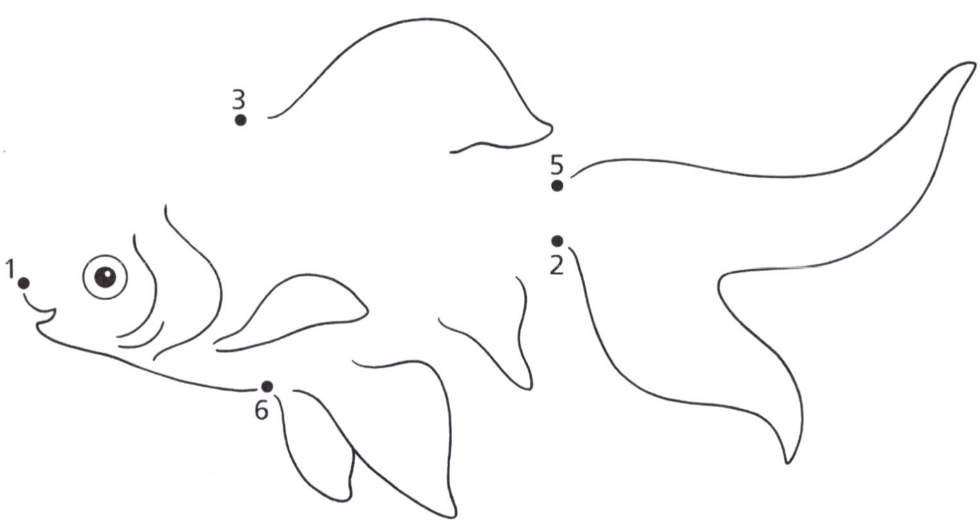

1. Listen and join the dots. **2.** Listen and colour.
Diff ⇩ L liest die Hörtexte selbst vor.

CD 1/ 25 – 26
KV 21 a-b
FC/WC 18 – 28, (1 – 7)

Role play: Rain, rain go away

1 **2**

1.

2.

3.

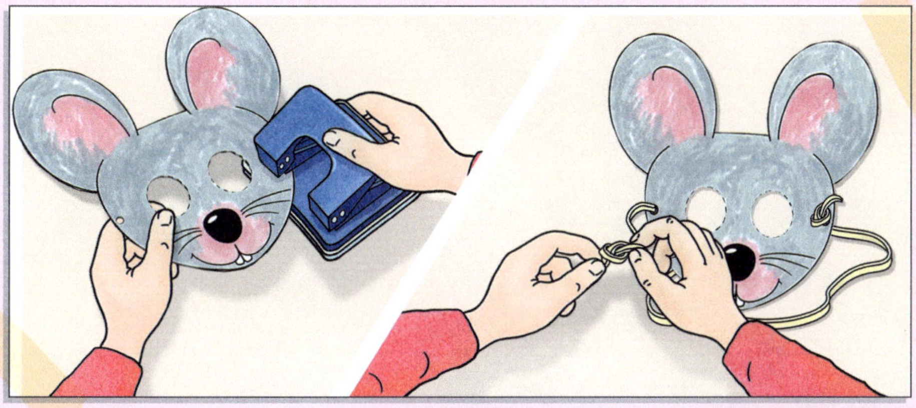

4.

1. Choose your pet and make your mask. **2.** Act it out.
Diff ⇩ SuS basteln nur die Maske und stellen diese vor.

CD 1/ 24
KV 22 a-e
SC 1 – 6

PORTFOLIO SEITE 74

Hobbies

1

2

3

1. Listen. 2. Listen and point.
3. Listen and number. What hobby is missing?
Diff ⇩ L liest die Hörtexte selbst vor.

CD 1/ 27 – 29
KV 23
FC 29 – 33

Ich kann meine Hobbys vorstellen.

Favourite hobbies 1

1

2

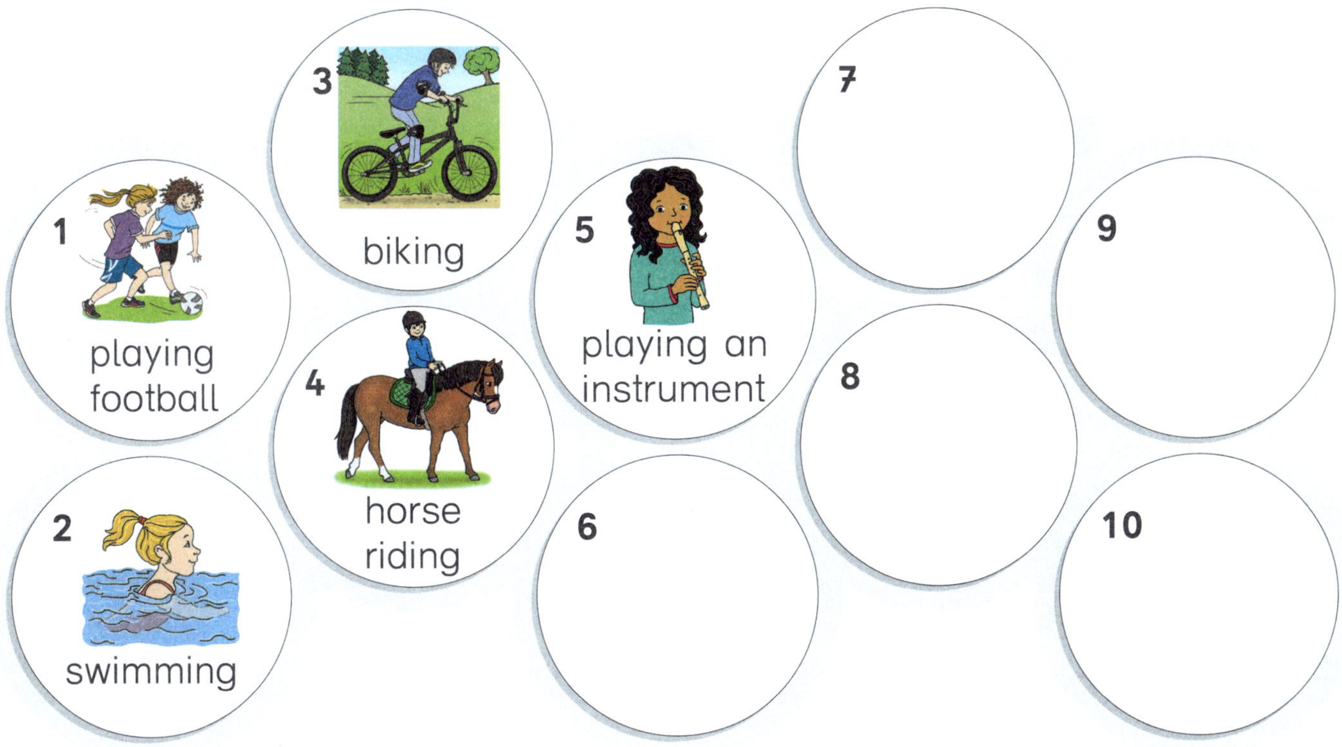

3

4

My hobby is ...

My hobbies are ...

1. Listen and point. 2. Listen and repeat.
3. Listen and match. 4. What about you? Talk to your partner.
Diff ⇑ SuS ergänzen Hobbys.

CD 1/30
KV 23, 24, 102
FC/WC 29–33

★ Ich kenne die Hobbywörter und kann meine Lieblingshobbys nennen.

Favourite hobbies 2

1

1:

2:

3:

4:

5:

2

I like ...

1. Listen and tick. **2.** What about you? Draw and present.
Diff ⇩ SuS stellen ihr Hobby im Einwortsatz vor.

CD 1/31 **KV** 25
FC/WC 29 – 33

★ Ich kann Hobbys nach Hörtext zuordnen und andere Kinder nach ihrem Hobby fragen.

What hobbies do you like?

1

2

3

I like ...

I don't like ...

name					
me					

1. Listen to the children. **2.** Listen again and fill in the table.
3. Ask three children. Fill in the table.
Diff ⇩ SuS befragen nur ein weiteres Kind.

CD 1/ 32 **KV** 27
FC/WC 29–33

The clapping game

1

2

1. Listen to the story. 2. Listen again. Clap and say the rhythm.

Diff ⇧ SuS geben die Geschichte auf Deutsch wieder.

Diff ⇩ L liest den Hörtext selbst vor.

CD 1/33 KV 28, 29

SC 7–12

FUN PAGE

Song: Boom, snap, clap! (traditional)

1 2

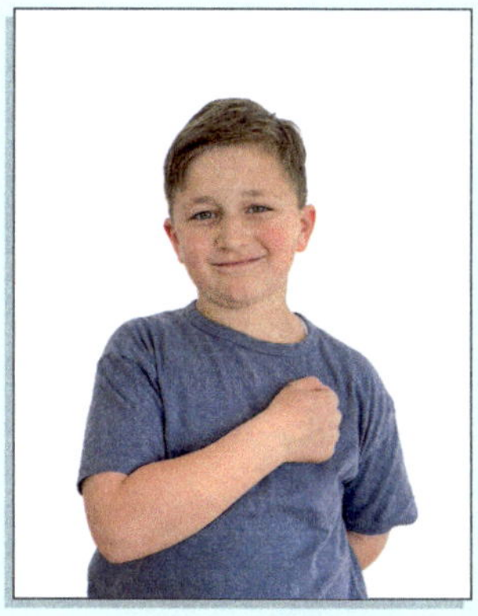

1. Listen. **2.** Listen again and do the rhythm.
Diff ⇧ SuS kreieren eigene Klatschreime.
Diff ⇩ L führt den Klatschreim selbst vor.

CD 1/ 34–35
KV 26, 30 a-b

PORTFOLIO SEITE 75

All about me

1

3

2

1. Listen. **2.** Listen and point. **3.** Listen and number.
Diff ⇑ SuS äußern sich frei zur Illustration.
Diff ⇓ L liest die Hörtexte selbst vor.

CD 1/ 36–38
KV 31
FC 34–39

★ Ich kenne die Begriffe für Familienmitglieder.

Family

1

2

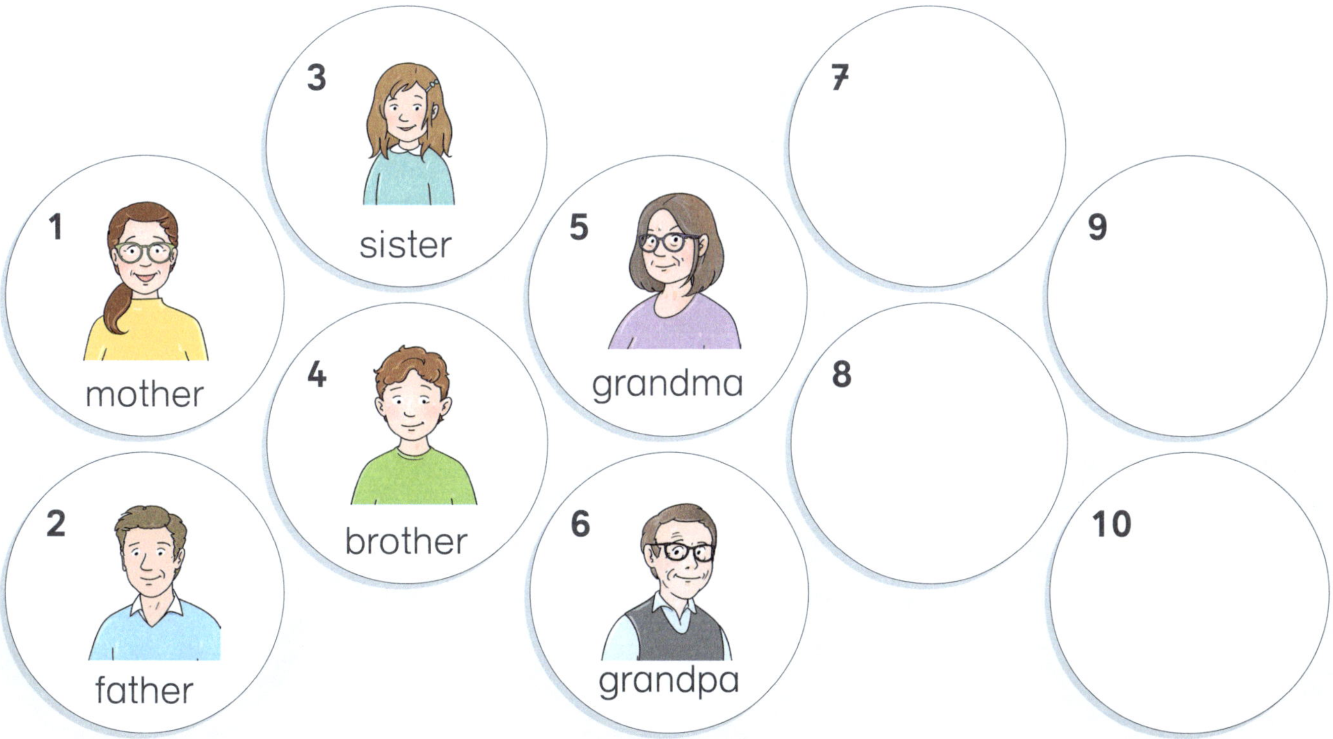

3

4

1. Listen and point. **2.** Listen and repeat. **3.** Listen and circle.
4. Say the lines.
Diff ⇑ SuS ergänzen Familienmitglieder. **Wdh.** colours, pets, hobbies

CD 1/ 39 **KV** 31, 32, 33
FC/WC 34–39, (1–7, 16–22, 29–33)

★ Ich kann ein Lied zum Thema Familie singen.

Song: My family (Wolle Kriwanek, Michael Schwarz, Jörg Orlamünder)

1

2

3

4

Aus rechtlichen Gründen können zum Lied und zur Story keine QR-Codes angeboten werden.

1. Listen to the song. **2.** Listen and sing along.
3. Make your own family song. **4.** Present your song.
Diff ⇩ SuS stellen ihre Familie im Einwortsatz vor.

CD 1/ 40 – 41
FC/WC 34 – 39

★ Ich kann eine Geschichte zum Thema Familie verstehen.

IT'S STORYTIME

The Frog family (Sarah Phillips)

1

2

1. Listen. **2.** Listen and number.

Diff ⇑ SuS geben die Geschichte auf Deutsch wieder.

Diff ⇓ L liest den Hörtext selbst vor.

CD 1/ 42 **KV** 34, 35

SC 13 – 18

Lots of families

1

2

1. Listen and fill in. **2.** Listen and number.
Diff ⇩ L liest den Hörtext selbst vor.
Wdh. colours, pets, numbers, hobbies

CD 1/ 43 – 44
KV 36
FC/WC 1 – 39

My poster

1

2

1. Make a poster about yourself. **2.** Present your poster.
Diff ⇑ SuS stellen ihr Poster digital unter Anleitung der L vor.
Diff ⇓ SuS präsentieren ihr Poster in Einwortsätzen.

KV 37
FC/WC 1–39

Food and drink

1 Listen.

2 Listen and point.

3 Listen and number.

4 What food and drink do you like? Talk to your partner.

Diff ⇑ SuS äußern sich frei zur Illustration.
Diff ⇓ L liest die Hörtexte selbst vor.

CD 1/ 45–46
KV 38, 42
FC 40–49

★ Ich kenne die Begriffe für die englischen Frühstückssachen.

Breakfast

1 Listen and point.

2 Listen and repeat.

3 Listen, read and number.

tea	butter	jam	toast	milk	orange juice
1	2	3	4	5	6

4 Write.

tea jam butter

FLORY'S MAGIC PHOTO ALBUM

More British food

1 Listen.

2 Listen and number.

3 What would you like to eat?

I would like to eat ...

Diff ⇧ SuS suchen nach weiteren Spezialitäten im Internet.
Diff ⇩ L liest die Hörtexte selbst vor.

CD 1/ 48–49
KV 44, 102

Numbers 1-10

1 Listen and point.

2 Listen and repeat.

1 one	3 three	5 five	7 seven	9 nine
2 two	4 four	6 six	8 eight	10 ten

3 Listen and colour the numbers.

4 Write the number words.

___________ ___________ ___________ ___________

★ Ich kann ein englisches Zahlenlied singen.

Song: Ten green bottles (traditional)

1 Listen. **2** Listen again and sing the song.

3 Listen again, look, and write the number word. You can look for help on page 37.

____

____

____

____

Diff ⇩ SuS singen nur die ersten vier Strophen.

CD 1/ 51–52
KV 46 a-b, 47
FC/WC 50–53, 23–28

My fruit porridge

1 Listen and look.

2 Make your own fruit porridge.

Body parts and feelings

1 Listen. **2** Listen and point.

3 Listen and number.

Diff ⇧ SuS äußern sich frei zur Illustration.
Diff ⇩ L liest die Hörtexte selbst vor.
Wdh. numbers

CD 1/ 54–55
KV 48, 52
FC 54–63

Body parts

1 Listen and point. **2** Listen and repeat.

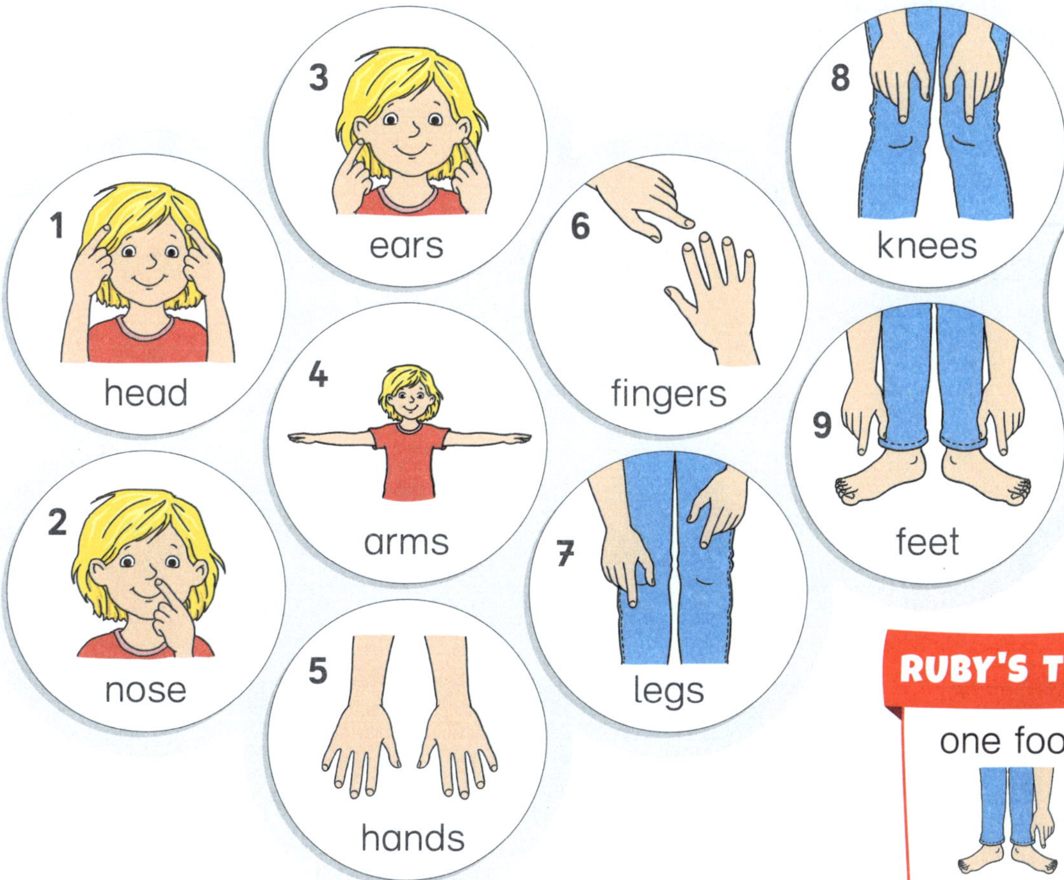

RUBY'S TIP

one foot – two feet

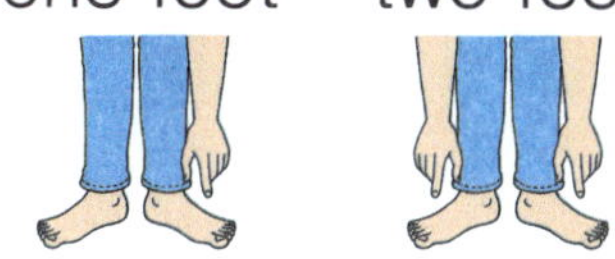

3 Listen, read and match.

head

toes

hands

4 Write.

nose

ears

legs

Song: The hokey cokey (traditional)

1 Listen. **2** Listen and do the movements.

3 Listen and sing along.

1

2

3

4

5

6

7

8

9

10

11

12

Diff ⇑ SuS singen und tanzen einzelne Strophen alleine vor.
Diff ⇓ L singt den Song selbst vor.

CD 1/ 57–58
FC/WC 57, 58, 60, 61
KV 54

Bumblebee in the forest

1 Listen to the story.

2 Listen and number.

3 What is the story about? Tell it in German.

Feelings

1 Listen and point.

2 Listen and repeat.

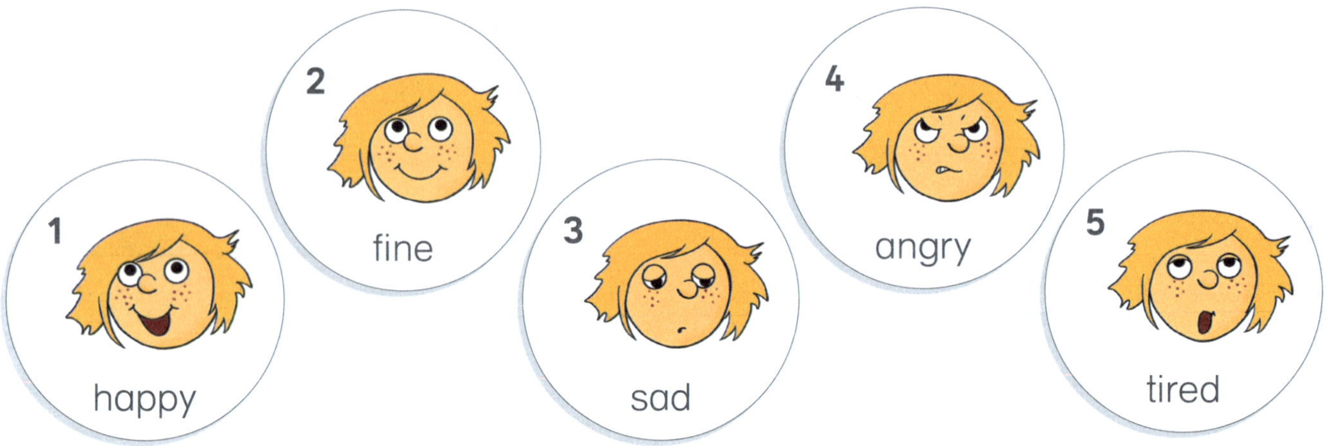

3 Listen and look at the pictures. Write the feelings.

4 Practise the dialogues.

Diff ⇧ SuS spielen weitere Gefühlssituationen nach.

CD 2/ 2
KV 50, 51, 56, 102
FC/WC 65–69

My monster

1 Roll your dice. Draw your monster.

2 Present your monster.

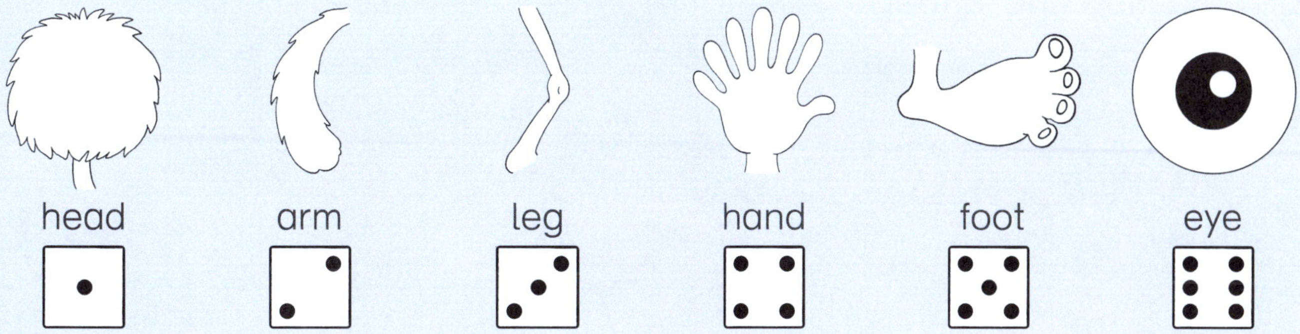

PORTFOLIO SEITE 78

Diff ⇧ SuS stellen ihr Poster digital unter Anleitung der L vor.
Diff ⇩ SuS präsentieren ihr Poster in Einwortsätzen.

KV 57

Farm animals

1 Listen and point.

2 Listen and number. Which farm animals are missing?

3 What can you see? Talk to your partner.

Diff ⇩ L liest die Hörtexte selbst vor.
Wdh. pets

CD 2/ 3–4
KV 58
FC 70–78

★ Ich kann die Farmtiere benennen und zählen.

Farm animals and colours

1 Listen and point. **2** Listen and repeat.

1

cow

2

pig

3

duck

4

horse

5

chicken

6

sheep

7
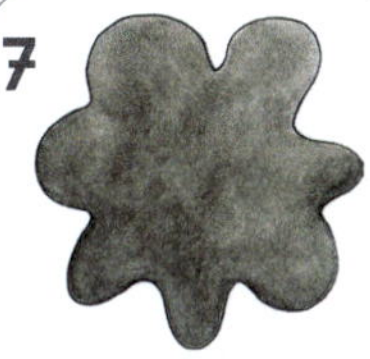
black

8

white

9

brown

RUBY'S TIP

one sheep  two sheep 

3 Look at page 46. How many farm animals can you see? Count and write.

	 cats	 sheep	 rabbits	 pigs	 chickens	 cows
I can see	2 / two					

Diff ⇑ SuS nennen ggf. weitere Farmtiere.
Diff ⇓ SuS arbeiten mit einem Partnerkind.
Wdh. colours, numbers

KV 58 – 62, 104
FC/WC 70 – 78, (23 – 28, 50 – 53)

Song: Old MacDonald (traditional)

1 Listen and point. **2** Listen and number.

3 Listen and sing the song.

4 Listen, read and match.

cluck cluck | woof woof | oink oink

baa baa | moo moo

Diff ⇑ SuS tragen einige Strophen auswendig vor.
Diff ⇓ L singt das Lied selbst vor.

CD 2 / 5–7
KV 63, 102
FC/WC 70–75

Farm animal fun

1 Listen and point.

2 Listen and number.

3 What is the story about? Tell it in German.

4 Read and tick.

	😊	☹
The dog says: "woof, woof"	X	
The cat says: "oink, oink"		
The pig says: "oink, oink"		
The chicken says: "baa baa"		
The cow says: "moo, moo"		

Diff ⇧ Aufgabe 3: SuS nennen die richtigen Tierlaute.
Diff ⇩ L liest den Hörtext selbst vor.

CD 2/ 8 **KV** 64
FC/WC 70 – 75
SC 25 – 30

On the farm

1 Listen and colour.

2 Look, match and write.

pig

chicken

duck

horse

Diff ⇩ SuS arbeiten mit einem Partnerkind.

CD 2/ 9
FC/WC 70 – 75

Farm animals – game

1 Play the game.

I can see a horse.

Clothes and weather

1 Listen. 2 Listen and point.

3 Listen and number.

4 What can you see? Talk to your partner.

There are two T-shirts.

Diff ⇧ SuS nennen die Farben der Kleidungsstücke.
Diff ⇩ L liest die Hörtexte selbst vor.

CD 2/ 10–11
KV 66, 70 a-b
FC 79–88

Clothes

1 Listen and point.

2 Listen and repeat.

3 Listen, match and colour.

Lina | Mike | Emily

Weather

1 Listen and point.

2 Listen and repeat.

3 Listen, read and tick.

☐ It's rainy.	☐ It's windy.	☐ It's snowy.
☐ It's sunny.	☐ It's foggy.	☐ It's cloudy.

Diff ⇩ L liest die Hörtexte selbst vor.

CD 2/ 13
KV 68, 69
FC/WC 89 – 98

Song: What's the weather like today? (Rozanne Lanczak)

1 Listen.

2 Listen and number the pictures.

3 Write the weather words.

4 Listen and sing the song.

1 

cloudy

Diff ⇧ SuS singen das Lied auswendig vor.
Diff ⇩ L liest den Hörtext selbst vor.

CD 2/ 14–15
KV 73
FC/WC 89–95

Aus rechtlichen Gründen kann zum Lied kein QR-Code angeboten werden.

FLORY'S MAGIC PHOTO ALBUM

Weather at London sights

1 Listen.

2 Listen and label.

~~Buckingham Palace~~

Tower Bridge London Eye

Big Ben Tower of London

Buckingham Palace

3 Talk about the weather in London. Listen and practise the dialogues.

Diff ⇧ SuS nennen weitere Sehenswürdigkeiten.
Diff ⇩ L liest die Hörtexte selbst vor.

CD 2/ 16–18
KV 74
FC/WC 89–94

Clothes and weather – game

1 Play the game.

I can see a jacket.

Diff ⇑ SuS nennen zusätzlich die Farbe und Anzahl der Kleidungsstücke.
Diff ⇓ SuS sprechen im Einwortsatz.

FC/WC 79–98
KV 72

PORTFOLIO SEITE 80

Seasons and friends

1 Listen. 2 Listen and point.

3 Listen and number.

4 What can you see? Talk to your partner.

Diff ⇩ L liest die Hörtexte selbst vor.

Wdh. weather

CD 2/ 19–20
KV 75
FC 99–107, 30, 31

Activities in the seasons

1 Listen and point.

1

spring

3

autumn

2

summer

4

winter

2 Listen and repeat.

5

sledging

8

skateboarding

6

flying a kite

9

ice-skating

7

eating ice cream

3 Listen, read and match.

Tim

Tina

Alex

I like flying a kite in autumn.

I like eating ice cream in summer.

I like skateboarding in spring.

Song: I like autumn

1 Listen.

2 Listen and write.

3 Listen and sing the song.

~~autumn~~	spring	summer	winter
~~autumn~~	spring	summer	winter

I like autumn. 2 x

Autumn is fun. 2 x

I like ______. 2 x

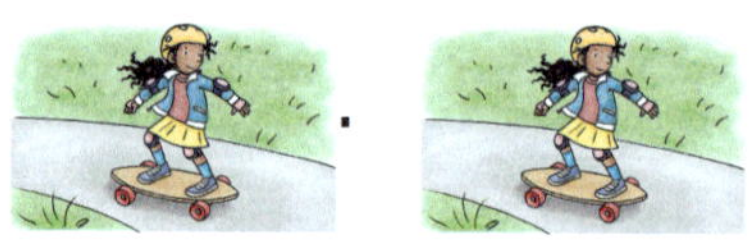

______ is fun. 2 x

I like ______. 2 x

______ is fun. 2 x

I like ______. 2 x

______ is fun. 2 x

Diff ⇧ SuS singen das Lied auswendig vor.
Diff ⇩ L liest den Hörtext selbst vor.

CD 2/ 22–23
KV 81 a-c
FC/WC 99–107, 30, 31

★ Ich kenne einige Eissorten und kann ein Eis bestellen.

Ordering an ice cream

1 Listen and point.

2 Listen and repeat.

1

chocolate

2

chocolate chip

3

vanilla

4

strawberry

5

lemon

6

7

8

9

10

3 Listen, read and number.

4 Practise the dialogue.

1 Hello, how many scoops would you like?

Here you are.

Thank you.

I'd like two scoops of lemon, please.

★ Ich kann einen Abzählreim verstehen und sprechen.

Rhyme: Five scoops of ice cream (traditional)

1 Listen to the rhyme.

2 Listen, write, and say the rhyme.

~~five~~	three	one	four	two

I have _five_ ______ scoops
of ice cream.

I have ______ scoops
of ice cream.

I have ______ scoops
of ice cream.

I have ______ scoops
of ice cream.

I have ______ scoop
of ice cream.

I have no scoops
of ice cream!

Diff ⇧ SuS tragen den Reim auswendig vor.
Diff ⇩ L liest den Hörtext selbst vor.

CD 2/ 25, 55
KV 81 a-c, 82

My ice cream

1 Draw your ice cream.

2 Do a role play.

Hello, how many scoops would you like?

I'd like … scoops of … , please.

Here you are.

Thank you.

Diff ⇧ SuS nehmen das Rollenspiel mit dem Tablet auf.
Diff ⇩ SuS lesen den Dialog ab.

KV 83
FC/WC 108 – 112

PORTFOLIO SEITE 81-82

FLORY'S MAGIC PHOTO ALBUM

Happy Halloween!

1 Listen.

2 Listen and number.

Diff ⇧ SuS äußern sich frei zu den Fotos.
Diff ⇩ L liest den Hörtext selbst vor.

CD 2/ 26 – 27
KV 84
FC 113 – 120

Song: Halloween rap (Renate Kreis, Christl Schultz)

1 Listen and point. **2** Listen and repeat.

3 Listen to the song. Read and colour.

4 Sing the song.

Trick or treat hey, hey, hey!

PORTFOLIO SEITE 83

Illustrationen: Karoline Kehr (Kürbis, Fledermaus hell, Friederike Schumann (Besen, Farbkleckse), Andrea Dölling (Kessel, Lagerfeuer, Fledermaus dunkel, Katze), Visuelle Lebensfreude (Vignetten), Oda Ruthe (restliche Bilder)

Christmas

1 Listen and point.

2 Listen and repeat.

3 Listen and match.

4 Which presents are missing? Circle.

Illustrationen: Karoline Kehr, Visuelle Lebensfreude (Vignetten)

Diff ⇧ SuS äußern sich frei zur Illustration.
Diff ⇩ L liest den Hörtext selbst vor.

CD 2/ 30
KV 87, 89, 91
FC/WC 121 – 131

Liebe Lehrerinnen und Lehrer, liebe Eltern,
diese Stickerbogenbeilage enthält die 28 Sticker für das Stickerbild auf Seite 70 im **One, two, fun! Workbook.** Für jede bearbeitete Seite, auf der die Figuren Bumblebee, Flory oder Ruby auftreten, können die Schülerinnen und Schüler anschließend einen Sticker vom Stickerbogen lösen und diesen in das Stickerbild einkleben. So entsteht nach und nach das fertige Bild mit den drei Lehrwerksfiguren.

p. 53

p. 63

p. 19

p. 7

p. 17

p. 29

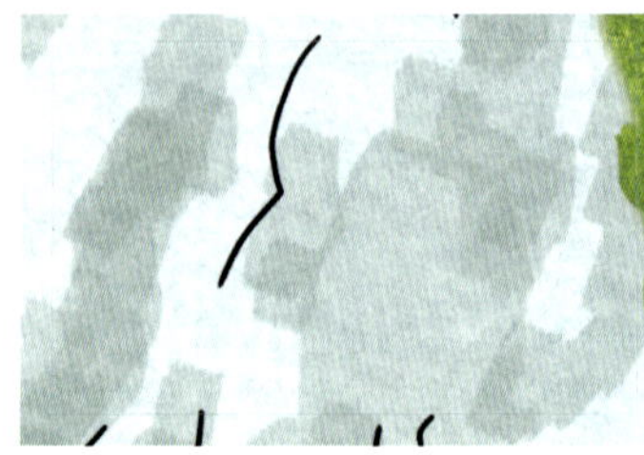

p. 41

p. 56

p. 13

p. 44

p. 49

p. 8

p. 57

p. 51

Illustrationen: Karoline Kehr (Bumblebee-Vorlage: Friederike Schumann, Ruby-Vorlage: Ulf Marckwort)

STICKERBOGEN

p. 36

p. 64

p. 47

p. 43

p. 31

p. 45

p. 4

p. 26

p. 15

p. 27

p. 9

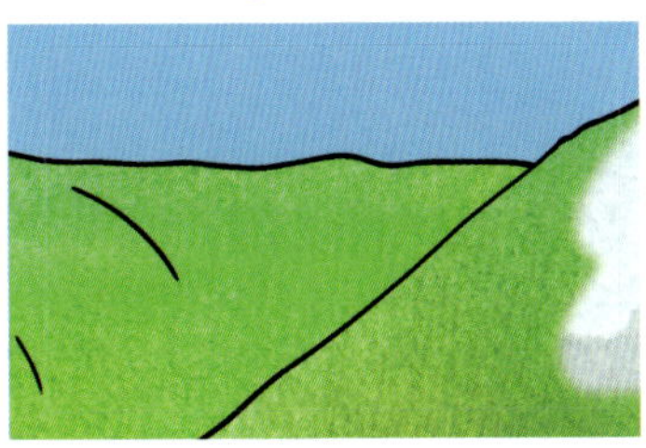

p. 39

p. 33

p. 21

We wish you a Merry Christmas (traditional)

1 What would you like for Christmas? Draw.

2 Ask your partner. Draw.

me — I would like … for Christmas.

my partner — I would like … for Christmas.

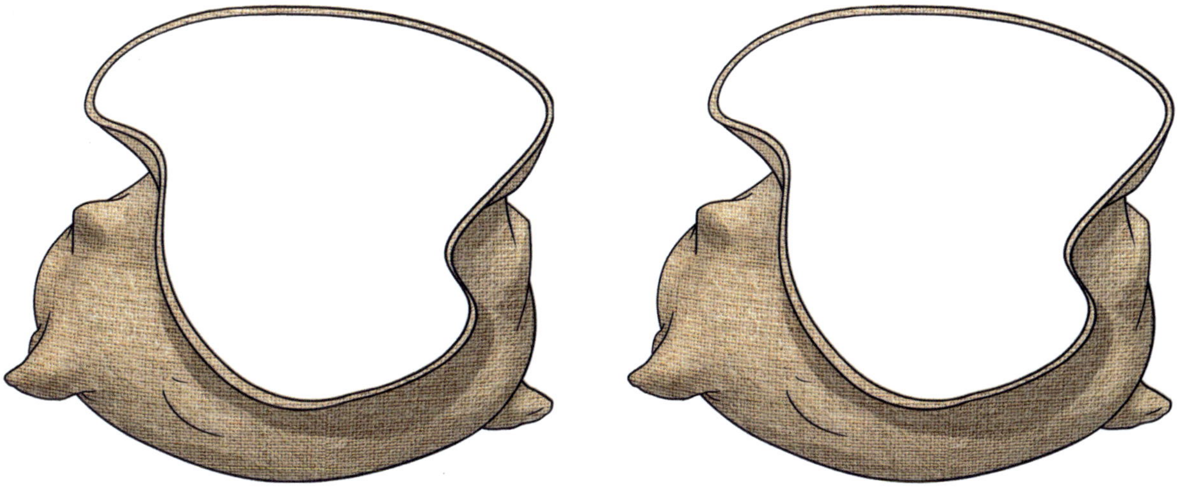

3 Listen to the song.

4 Listen and sing the song.

Diff ⇑ SuS singen das Lied alleine vor.

Illustrationen: Karoline Kehr (Säcke), Friederike Schumann (Weihnachtsmann), Ulf Markwort (Baum+Geschenke), Visuelle Lebensfreude (Vignetten)

CD 2/ 31 – 32
KV 87 – 93, 102, 104
FC/WC 121 – 131

PORTFOLIO SEITE 84

Happy Easter!

1 Listen and point.

2 Listen and repeat.

1  Easter eggs

2  candy

3  Easter bunny

4  lamb

5  chocolate eggs

6  basket

7  carrots

8  chick

3 Listen and say the rhyme.

Easter Surprise (traditional)

 ,

 and  ,

 ,

For me and you.

 ,

Candy sweet,

 ,

Are good to eat.

 ,

Pretty and funny,

But ...

Where, o where is the Easter bunny?

Illustrationen: Karoline Kehr (Eier Aufg. 3 +Kopfzeile), Andrea Dölling (Lamm), Ulf Markwort (Küken), Visuelle Lebensfreude (Vignetten), Friederike Schumann (restliche Bilder)

Diff ⇧ SuS tragen den Reim auswendig vor.
Diff ⇩ L liest den Hörtext selbst vor.

PORTFOLIO SEITE 85

CD 2/ 33
KV 94 – 97
FC/WC 132 – 139

Happy birthday!

1 Listen and point.

2 Listen and repeat.

3 Listen and sing along.

4 Read, write, and draw. How old are you?

My birthday

I am ________ years old.

This is my birthday cake.

Diff ⇧ SuS äußern sich frei zur Illustration.

Illustrationen: Visuelle Lebensfreude (Vignetten), Friederike Schumann (Torte Kopfzeile), Andrea Dölling (restliche Bilder)

CD 2/ 34 – 35
KV 98 – 100
FC/WC 140 – 144

PORTFOLIO SEITE 86

One, two, fun! – Stickerbild

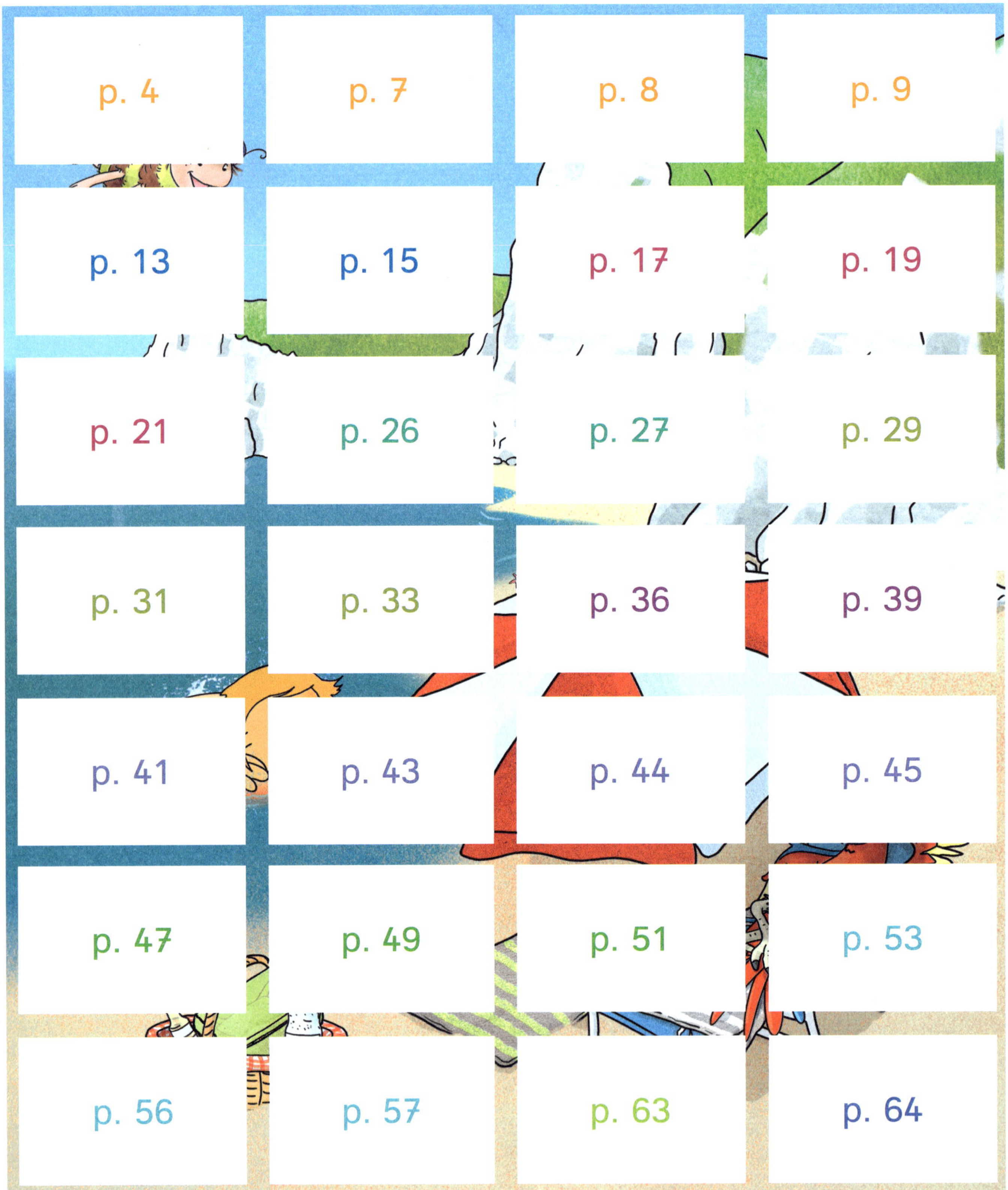

Illustrationen: Karoline Kehr

Ich heiße:

____

Zuhause spreche ich diese Sprachen:

____

____

Mit meinen Freunden spreche ich folgende Sprachen:

____

____

Diese Sprachen kenne ich zum Beispiel aus dem Urlaub, Radio oder Internet:

____

____

Ich möchte gerne folgende Sprachen noch lernen:

____

____

Illustrationen: Karoline Kehr (Computer), Friederike Schumann (Koffer, Globus), Andrea Dölling (restliche Bilder)

Das kann ich schon – Hello

1 Ich kann meine Mitschüler begrüßen und nach dem Namen fragen.

2 Ich kann diese Farben auf Englisch sagen.

3 Ich kann das Lied *I can sing a rainbow* singen.

4 Ich kenne ein Land in dem Englisch gesprochen wird.

Illustrationen: Markus Humbach (Regenbogen), Isabelle Metzen (USA-Flagge), Friederike Schumann (restliche Bilder)

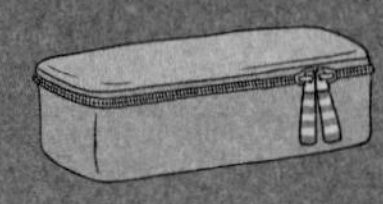

Das kann ich schon – At school

1 Ich kann diese Schulgegenstände auf Englisch nennen.
Male deine Lieblingswörter aus.

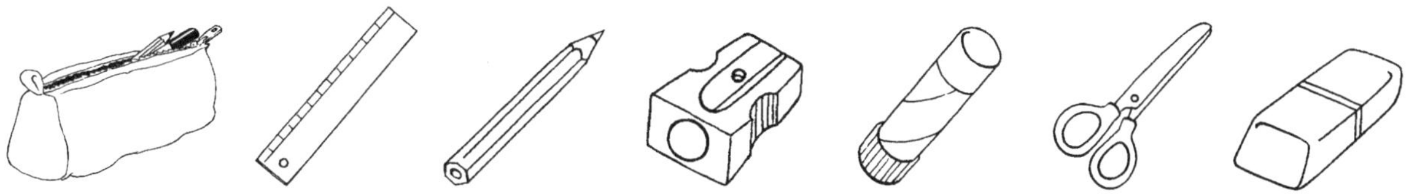

☐ ☐ ☐ ☐ ☐ ☐ ☐

2 Ich kann etwas zur Schule in Großbritannien erzählen.
Male, was du dir behalten hast.

3 Ich kann den *One, two, fun* Rap singen.

Illustrationen: Andrea Dölling (grünes Mäppchen), Ulf Marckwort (Mäppchen), Oda Ruthe (restliche Bilder)

Das kann ich schon – Pets

1 Ich kann diese Haustiere auf Englisch nennen.
Male deine Lieblingswörter aus.

☐ ☐ ☐ ☐ ☐ ☐ ☐

2 Ich kann sagen, welche Haustiere ich mag und welche nicht.

3 Ich kann diese Zahlen auf Englisch nennen.

6 ☐ 1 ☐ 2 ☐

4 ☐ 3 ☐ 5 ☐

4 Ich kann den *One, two* Reim aufsagen.

Illustrationen: Andrea Dölling (bunter Wellensittich), Oda Ruthe (restliche Bilder)

Das kann ich schon – Hobbies

1 Ich kann diese Hobbys auf Englisch nennen.
Male deine Lieblingswörter aus.

2 Ich kann mich mit jemandem über meine Hobbys unterhalten.

a) Ich kann nach einem Hobby fragen.

b) Ich kann meine Hobbys benennen.

3 Ich kann die Geschichte *The clapping game* verstehen und den Rhythmus mitklatschen.

4 Ich kann das Lied *Boom, snap, clap* singen und mit Bewegungen begleiten.

Illustrationen: Andrea Dölling (Mädchen mit Blockflöte), Juliane Assies (Radfahren), Oda Ruthe (restliche Bilder)

Das kann ich schon – All about me

1 Ich kann diese Familienmitglieder auf Englisch nennen.

2 Ich kann meine Familie vorstellen.

3 Ich kann das Lied *My family* singen.

Illustrationen: Juliane Assies

Das kann ich schon – Food and drink

1 Ich kann diese Wörter rund ums Frühstück auf Englisch nennen.

2 Ich kann mich mit jemandem über das Thema Frühstück unterhalten.

a) Ich kann nach dem Lieblingsfrühstück fragen.

b) Ich kann mein Lieblingsfrühstück benennen.

3 Ich kann das Lied *Ten green bottles* singen.

Illustrationen: Karoline Kehr (Toast), Oda Ruthe (Butter), Friederike Schumann (Milch), Andrea Dölling (restliche Bilder)

Das kann ich schon – Body parts and feelings

1 Ich kann diese Körperteile auf Englisch nennen.

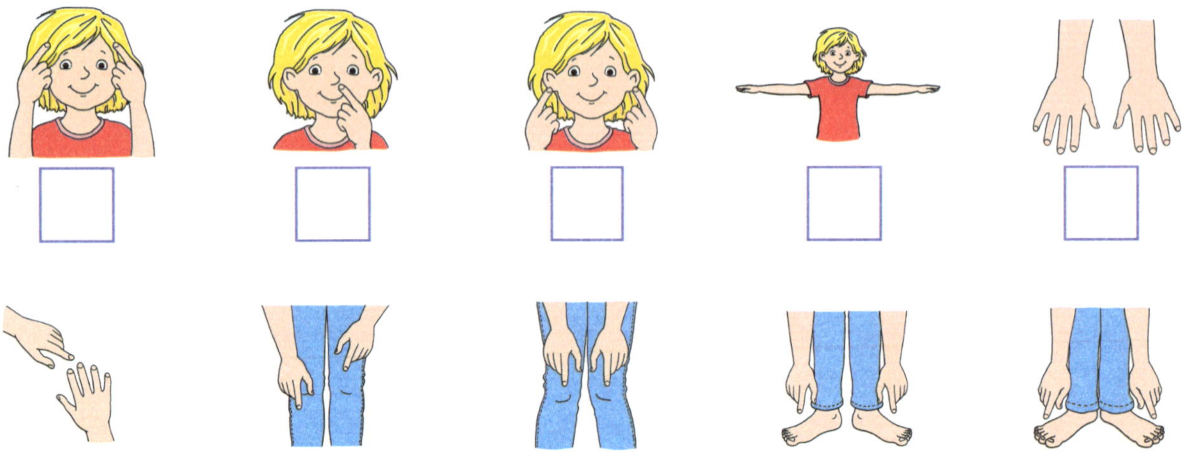

2 Ich kann die Körperteile eines Monsters beschreiben.
Male dein Monster.

3 Ich kann diese Gefühle auf Englisch benennen.

Illustrationen: Andrea Dölling (Körperteile), Karoline Kehr (Flory Bilder), Oda Ruthe (Monster)

Das kann ich schon – Farm animals

1 Ich kann diese Farmtiere auf Englisch nennen.
Male deine Lieblingswörter aus.

2 Ich kann die Farbe eines Farmtieres beschreiben.

3 Ich kann die Anzahl der Farmtiere abzählen.

4 Ich kann das Lied *Old MacDonald* singen.

Illustrationen: Andrea Dölling (weißes Schaf), Oda Ruthe (restliche Bilder)

Das kann ich schon – Clothes and weather

1 Ich kann diese Kleidungsstücke auf Englisch nennen.

2 Ich kann diese Wetterlagen auf Englisch nennen.

3 Ich kann beschreiben, welche Kleidung jemand trägt.

4 Ich kann das Lied *What's the weather like today?* singen.

Illustrationen: Karoline Kehr (Jeans), Ulf Marckwort (Kappe), Oda Ruthe (Kinder, Schuhe), Friederike Schumann (neblig, T-Shirt, windig), Andrea Dölling (restliche Bilder)

Das kann ich schon – Seasons and friends

1 Ich kann diese Jahreszeiten auf Englisch nennen.

2 Ich kann diese Aktivitäten auf Englisch nennen.

3 Ich kann das Lied *I like autumn* singen.

Illustrationen: Andrea Dölling (Eis essen, Drachen steigen lassen)
Oda Ruthe (Jahreszeiten), Friederike Schumann (restliche Bilder)

Das kann ich schon – Seasons and friends

4 Ich kann diese Eissorten auf Englisch benennen.

5 Ich kann mein Lieblingseis bestellen.

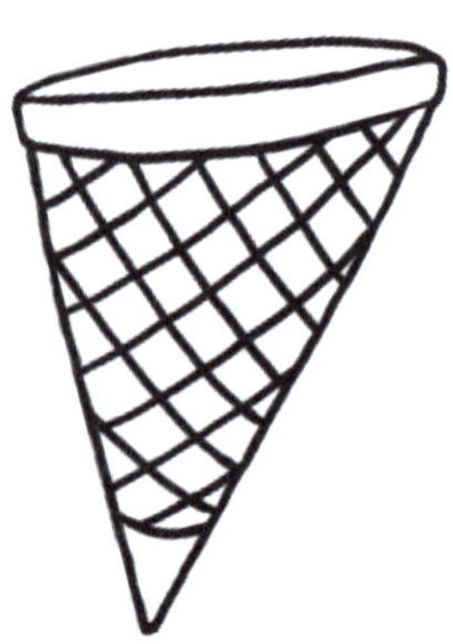

Illustrationen: Gabie Hilgert (Eiswaffel), Oda Ruthe (Eis), Friederike Schumann (Eissorten)

Das kann ich schon – Halloween

1 Ich kann diese Halloweenwörter auf Englisch nennen.
Male deine Lieblingswörter aus.

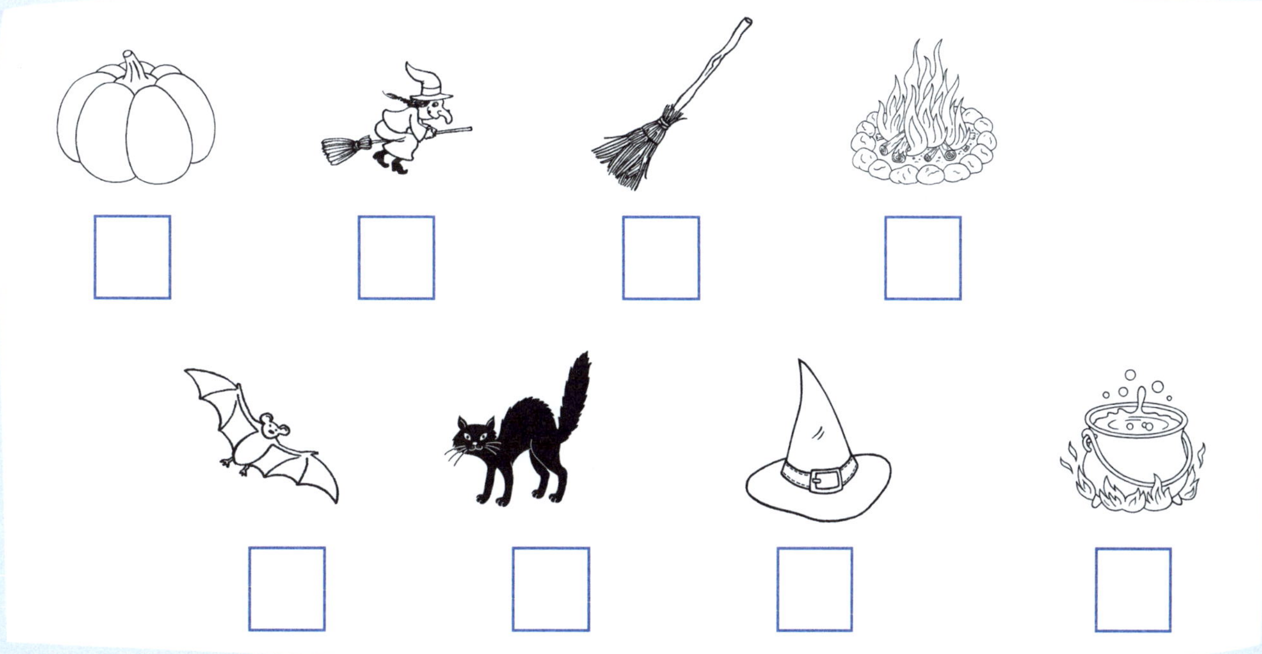

2 Ich kann etwas zum Halloweenfest erzählen.
Male was du dir behalten hast.

3 Ich kann den *Halloween rap* singen.

Illustrationen: Karoline Kehr (Kürbis), Oda Ruthe (restliche Bilder)

Das kann ich schon – Christmas

1 Ich kann diese Weihnachtswörter auf Englisch nennen.
Male deine Lieblingswörter aus.

2 Ich kann sagen, was ich mir zu Weihnachten wünsche.

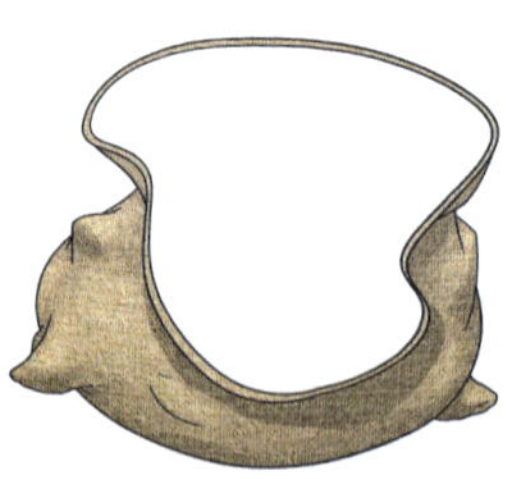

3 Ich kann das Lied *We wish you a Merry Christmas* singen.

Illustrationen: Juliane Assies (Ball), Carmen Hochmann (Roller), Karoline Kehr (Sack), Ulf Marckwort (Computerspiel), Friederike Schumann (Weihnachtsmann), Oda Ruthe (restliche Bilder)

Das kann ich schon – Easter

1 Ich kann diese Osterwörter auf Englisch nennen.
Male deine Lieblingswörter aus.

2 Ich kann den *Easter surprise* Reim sprechen.

Illustrationen: Andrea Dölling (Lamm), Karoline Kehr (Osterei), Ulf Marckwort (Karotten), Oda Ruthe (restliche Bilder)

Das kann ich schon – Birthday

1 Ich kann diese Geburtstagswörter auf Englisch nennen.
Male deine Lieblingswörter aus.

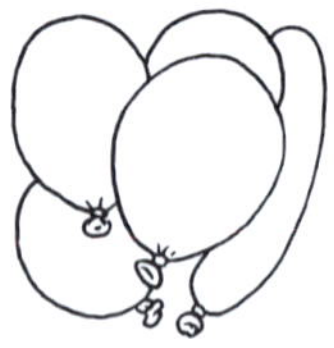

2 Ich kann das Lied *Happy Birthday* singen.

3 Ich kann sagen, wie alt ich bin.

Illustrationen: Andrea Dölling (Torten s/w), Ulf Marckwort (Luftballons), Oda Ruthe (Kerzen), Friederike Schumann (Torte bunt), Juliane Assies (restliche Bilder)

So verstehe und spreche ich Englisch

Hörverstehen

1. Ich schaue auf die Bilder.

2. Ich schaue auf das Gesicht und die Bewegungen meiner Lehrkraft.

3. Ich frage nach, wenn ich etwas nicht verstehe.

4. Ich höre den Hörtext mehrmals an.

Sprechen

1. Ich bin mutig und spreche mit.

2. Ich benutze die Wörter in den Sprechblasen.

Illustrationen: Juliane Assies

Open your workbooks at page ..., please.

Take care!

Let's play ...

Let's sing ...

Have a nice day!

Point to ...

Work with a partner.

Good morning.

Work in a group with three other children.

Listen to ...

Please be quiet.

See you!

 Illustrationen: Juliane Assies

May I go to the toilet, please?
I need help, please.

I don't have …
Here you are.
Thank you.
You're welcome.

Excuse me, can you say it again, please?
Yes, of course. …

Colours

red .... 

orange...... 

yellow ...... 

green .... 

blue .... 

purple ..... 

pink......... 

School things

ruler .... 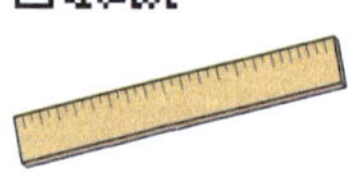

pencil........... 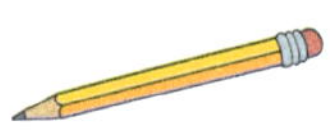

sharpener .... 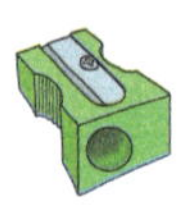

glue stick .... 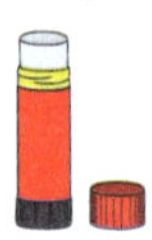

scissors .... 

rubber .... 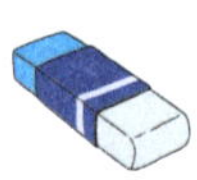

pencil case ..... 

school bag ..... 

Pets

cat 

dog 

mouse 

rabbit 

fish 

budgie 

hamster 

Numbers 1-6

one 1

two 2

three 3

four 4

five 5

six 6

Hobbies

playing football 

swimming 

biking 

horse riding 

playing an instrument 

Family

father 

mother 

sister 

brother 

grandma 

grandpa 

Breakfast

baked beans 

sausages 

tea 

milk 

orange juice 

toast 

jam 

butter 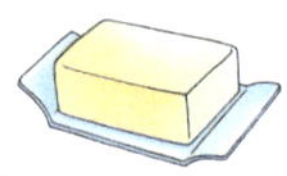

eggs 

tomatoes 

Numbers 7-10

seven 7

eight 8

nine 9

ten 10

Body parts

head .... 

nose .... 

ears .... 

arms .. 

hands .... 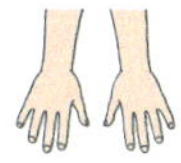

fingers .. 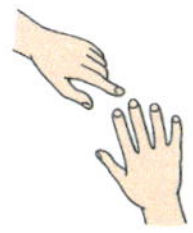

legs .... 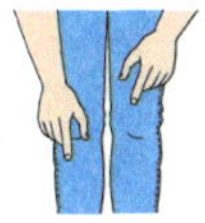

knees ..... 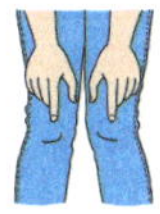

foot/feet .. 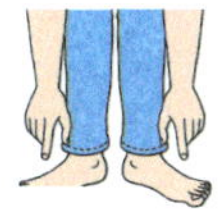

toes ... 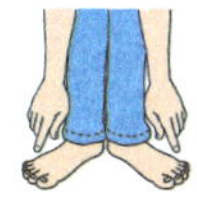

eyes .... 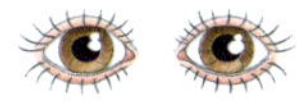

Feelings

happy .... 

fine .... 

sad .... 

angry ..... 

tired ...... 

Farm animals

cow .... 

pig ..... 

duck .... 

horse .... 

chicken .... 

sheep .... 

Colours

black ......

white ......

brown ......

Weather and clothes

cloudy ....

rainy ......

windy ....

snowy ......

sunny ....

foggy ......

perfect ....

woolly hat ......

scarf ......

gloves ......

Clothes

T-shirt ....

jeans ....

skirt ....

pullover ......

jacket ....

socks ....

shoes ....

shorts ......

hat ....

boots ......

Seasons

spring ......

summer ......

autumn ......

winter ......

Activities with friends

sledging ....

flying a kite ....

eating ice cream ....
skateboarding ....

ice-skating ....

Ice cream

chocolate ....

chocolate chip ....

vanilla ....
strawberry ....

lemon ....

Halloween

pumpkins ..

steeple hats ..

bats ....

witches .....

burning fire .....

black cats ..

broomsticks ..

cauldron ....

Christmas

Father Christmas ....
scooter ....

presents .....

chocolates ..

ball ....
cards ....

toy blocks ...

sack ......

computer game .....
reindeer ....

book ....

Easter

Easter eggs .... 

candy ......  

Easter bunny ...... 

lamb .... 

chocolate eggs .... 

basket .... 

carrots .... 

chick .... 

Birthday

birthday party .... 

birthday cake ...... 

candles .... 

birthday cards .... 

birthday presents .... 

balloons .... 

Texte soweit nicht anders angegeben: Karen B. Finck, Elke Neudeck, Ute Schwickert
S. 65: Renate Kreis, Christl Schultz: *Halloween rap.* Songs, Rhymes and Poems - Seasons and Festivals, Schroedel Verlag, Hannover, 2001, S.9 © Westermann Bildungsmedien Verlag GmbH, Braunschweig

Musiknachweis QR-Codes:
S. 12: One, two, fun! School things rap ℗ © Westermann Bildungsmedien Verlag. **S. 18:** One, two rhyme ℗ © Westermann Bildungsmedien Verlag. **S. 27:** Boom, snap, clap! Text/Musik: traditionell ℗ © Westermann Bildungsmedien Verlag. **S. 38:** Ten green bottles. Text/Musik: tradtitionell ℗ © Westermann Bildungsmedien Verlag. **S. 42:** The hokey cokey. Text/Musik: traditionell ℗ © Westermann Bildungsmedien Verlag. **S. 48:** Old MacDonald. Text/Musik: traditionell ℗ © Westermann Bildungsmedien Verlag. **S. 55:** What's the weather like today? Musik: traditionell ℗ © Westermann Bildungsmedien Verlag. **S. 60:** I like autumn. Musik: traditionell. ℗ © Westermann Bildungsmedien Verlag. **S. 67:** We wish you a Merry Christmas. Text/Musik: traditionell. Arrangement: Claus Hartisch, tonvision, Königslutter. ℗ © Westermann Bildungsmedien Verlag. **S. 69:** Happy birthday. Text/Musik: traditionell ℗ © Westermann Bildungsmedien Verlag.

Sänger/Sängerinnen:
Pete Cousins, Anna Chloe Moorey, Chris Stanchev & Jemima Dicker
Musikprodukion: Holger Buhr, Musikverlag db music (als Eigenproduktion für den Westermann Bildungsmedien Verlag)
Arrangement, Komposition und Produktion aller Raps, Reime und Songs soweit nicht anders angegeben:
Holger Buhr, Musikverlag db music
Gesamtproduktion und Mastering: Stephan Dupré
Alle Rap-, Reim-, Song-, Gedichttexte soweit nicht anders angegeben: Karen B. Finck, Elke Neudeck, Ute Schwickert